Why I
Miss You

1

When I hear the song

"____,"

it always reminds me of you.

2

Eating

____

is just not the same without you.

3

Drinking

____

is way less

____

without you.

4

When I pass by

____,

I always remember that time we

____.

5

Sometimes I can hear you
in my head, telling me

____.

6

I love how whenever we

____,

it's like no time has passed.

7

Whenever I get a call from you, I

____.

8

They should make a Broadway musical
about us and call it

"____."

9

I probably think about you

____

times a day.

10

When you're not around, I

____

too much.

11

When you're not around, I don't

____

nearly enough!

12

If you were a children's book, you'd be

____.

13

I love telling people about how you

____.

14

I miss getting together
spur-of-the-moment to

____.

15

It's always so

when we first see each other again!

16

Whenever I smell

____,

I think of you.

17

I wish we could spend

____

together.

18

I miss the way you always

____.

19

I miss the way you never

____.

20

We should talk on the phone and

---

at the same time.

21

without you is just plain boring!

22

I spotted a

____

and it reminded me of you.

23

Next time we hang out, let's

____

until

____.

24

Knowing you makes me appreciate

____

even more.

25

In your absence, I've had to learn how to

____

by myself.

26

Unfortunately, I still

haven't learned how to

____

like you.

27

I love how your

____

is a little different every time
we see each other.

28

I love how your

____

never changes.

29

and

should play us in a movie.

30

I miss dragging you to

____.

31

I hope you sometimes miss my

_______________________________________.

32

I am sure you don't miss my

____!

33

Let's make a point to

____

each other every

____.

34

I can't wait to take you

____

the next time we get together.

35

Our texts could make a really

____

novel.

36

After we see each other

I always have lots of

____.

37

I love how you always seem

to call me right when

____.

38

If you were an emoji, you'd be

____.

39

I miss hearing you

____.

40

We should start a long-distance

____

club.

41

Remember how we always used to

______________________________________?

I miss that.

42

Whenever I hear people say

"____,"

I think of you.

43

Have I told you lately how much I

____

you?

44

Let's pretend we still

____.

45

If you were a good luck charm, you'd be

____.

46

Please don't forget me when you

____.

47

Being

is so us.

48

When it comes to

______________________________________,

you rock.

49

Believe it or not, I even miss your

____.

50

It's so much fun being your

____.

Ugh, I miss you!